Roger Vivier

Translated from the French by Jane Brenton

First published in Great Britain in 1999
by Thames and Hudson Ltd, London

Copyright © 1998 Éditions Assouline, Paris

British Library Cataloguing-in-Publication Data
A catalogue record for this book is available from
the British Library

ISBN 0-500-01926-6

Printed and bound in Italy

Roger Vivier

Colombe Pringle

Thames and Hudson

t he stiletto heel that lends that dramatic 'final touch to the silhouette', whose audaciously plunging lines were intended originally to complement Christian Dior's designs of 1954, we owe to Roger Vivier – and by 'we', in this context, I mean not only all of us women who want to put on a few extra inches in height, and know we have the poise to carry it off, but also all the multitude of men for whom these exclamation marks are magnets to the eye, and an exquisite punctuation of their dreams.

We have him to thank also for the high thigh boots that, during the sixties, so flatteringly encased women's legs in bold shiny black vinyl – the type worn by Brigitte Bardot as she perched on a Harley Davidson and sang of her need to be alone. They were designed to accompany the collections of Yves Saint Laurent and Emanuel Ungaro. Musketeer's boots, black ginza legwear, patent-leather stocking-shoes, boots of clear plastic with platform sole and square heel – the man who liked to describe himself simply as a *bottier* ('bootmaker') came up with a thousand and one different ways of emphasizing the legs, which were flaunted unashamedly and accompanied by the most minimal of skirts to maximize the effect. With typical audacity and wit, he also anticipated the imminent arrival on the womenswear scene of the trouser suit, a liberating garment to which his jazzy ankle boots were to provide the perfect complement. Vivier developed the 'moon boot' specially for the singer Françoise Hardy who, in her guise of space explorer, was already wearing a form of pants suit. She was the lunar princess, the toast of France, icon of an age in which fashion had set foot on the surface of the moon. John Lennon, too, wore moon boots. He had a pair made in trendy black satin, with square heels studded with rhinestones, for stage appearances; the fans were ecstatic, transported almost to a state of frenzy. And Rudolf Nureyev, catapulted into the salons of the free world, performed his first entrechats in the West in crocodile thigh boots.

The invention in the mid-sixties of practical, well-engineered high heels, enabling the tribe of urban Amazons to adopt the look of the 'intrepid independent woman' even before they had properly formulated their desire for liberation, was once again down to Roger Vivier. In *Belle de Jour*, the inimitable Catherine Deneuve embarked on her journey into adultery wearing those famous low-heeled pumps with the square silver buckles. Women flocked to follow her example, craving, if nothing else, then at least this essential accessory for the errant wife. In a single year, two hundred thousand pairs of the must-have model walked out of shops all over the world. The boutique on the Rue François Iᵉʳ in Paris was always packed. Challenging the conventions head-on, yet always respecting the golden rules of equilibrium, Roger Vivier sculpted a range of heels with bold yet pure lines: 'torpedo', 'Punch', 'comma', *'choc'*, 'ball', 'bobbin', 'cabriole', 'can-can'. Each season had its extravagances; each collection sparked its own small revolution inside the fragile temple of fashion.

He was the master of frivolity. In the thirties, breaking with the conventional wisdom that shoes should be made of kid and always in sober colours, Vivier allowed his virtuoso invention free rein, decking Mistinguett's feet in spangles and Josephine Baker's in pendant crystals. He produced his own individual and innovative take on the embroidered slippers fashionable at the court of Louis XV. Three decades later, he persuaded Marlene Dietrich to walk on rhinestone-studded balls, raised insolently above mere mortals, her foot capriciously arched inside a plain black-satin high-heeled pump. And it was Roger Vivier who 'conveyed' the young Princess Elizabeth to her coronation on his 'gold kid-skin sandals, their arabesque straps and heels studded with rubies [in fact, ruby-coloured garnets], the stone that symbolizes marriage to one's country, designed to match her crown'. A regal design for a testing day. A challenge, too, for the shoemaker, who developed the prototype in his workshop at Mougins (Alpes-Maritimes), inventing a double sole to supply the future Queen Elizabeth II with a stature equal to her rank.

besieged by the most famous women in the world, the man journalists called the 'heel king' was nevertheless hugely conscious of the restrictions and elitism of the world of made-to-measure. In 1953, as Dior's accredited designer, he inaugurated a range of shoes made under licence by Charles Jourdan in Romans-sur-Isère (Drôme). The models bore the legend '*Christian Dior créé par* [created by] *Roger Vivier*'. This was a first for the inventor of the New Look, who had never before allowed his name to be used in association with that of any other designer, and it represented a decisive moment in the democratization of fashion. A few years later, Vivier took another step along this road. Ready-to-wear was where the real money lay, and although that branch of fashion had made great strides, 'it lacked accessories, the ultimate test of true refinement', as the magazine *Elle* was to declare in July 1959 in announcing the great event marked by the arrival in six Paris shops of 'exclusive high-fashion models, carefully designed in every detail to complement the new fashion line'. What is more, they were on sale at affordable prices. This new departure represented for Roger Vivier the achievement of 'one of my greatest ambitions' since he had first started making shoes – that of being 'at every woman's feet'.

Vivier always used the more classical term *soulier* when he spoke of shoes, following the example of Christian Dior. 'Can you imagine talking of Marie-Antoinette's *chaussures* [footwear]?' Dior once said to him. Roger Vivier never forgot it. He was always quick to acknowledge the master couturier's influence – he worked with him right up to his death in October 1957 – but even before the two men met, Vivier was already recognized as the preeminent designer of shoes for women.

a Parisian through and through, Roger Vivier was born in November 1907 in the 8th arrondissement. At fifteen, an age at which a young person's ideas are still fluid, he knew he had no particular fondness for the classical disciplines. Equally, there was nothing in his background to direct him towards a career in the arts – his father managed restaurants – and yet it was the music hall that drew him. He used to spend his evenings hanging around backstage and taking walk-on parts at the Théâtre de Belleville. In the end, he was not to make a career on the boards, but always retained a feel for the drama and dazzle of stage costumes as well as that love of decoration that became his signature. During the day, he attended sculpture classes at the Ecole des Beaux-Arts, developing an appreciation of form and volume that was to inform his future designs. He was flirting even then with fashion, and produced a number of handkerchiefs painted with exuberant arabesques. Alas, they have not survived: because he used watercolours, the pattern faded the moment it was washed.

Roger's parents had died before he was ten years old, and family friends offered him the chance to train for a career just as the Roaring Twenties were getting into their stride. 'They had a small shoe factory on the outskirts of Paris. There I was initiated into all the various stages of manufacture before going on to make the first models of my own. Since then I have worked continuously. And I've always kept a close eye on fashion. I pick up on its vibrations.' It was thus at the tender age of seventeen that Roger Vivier began to learn the rudiments of his future craft, and was inculcated into the art of bootmaking by master craftsmen. He was subsequently commissioned by the firm of Laboremus, Parisian subsidiary of the German tanners Heyl-Liebenau, to promote Rhineland leathers: quality products that suffered from a drab conformity of design, which Vivier was to dispel utterly with his use of new and brilliant colours. Bursting with ideas, he would spend his evenings carving out designs for heels and uppers, giving form to his fantasies in a delicious 'fever of excitement'.

●

I n 1937, Roger Vivier opened his first shop selling exclusive models for private customers. That was in the Rue Royale, one of the most prestigious addresses in Paris. His work was photographed by Brassaï and created a stir among other shoemakers. He began to send his designs to major shoe manufacturers all over the world. The ideas he submitted were always in advance of the current fashion, often witty send-ups of prevailing artistic trends. For example, there was his outrageous *Automatique*, a model which – in a reference to the Surrealists – had a telephone dial mounted on its upper. Or the revolutionary cork-soled platform shoe adopted by Schiaparelli, which Delman, his biggest customer in the United States, with whom he had just signed an exclusive contract, had turned down with a stinging 'Are you crazy?' – only to invite him to visit New York the following year. That trip to the New World would mark a crucial stage in Roger Vivier's life, enabling him to forge friendships with a number of artists whose works remained in his possession for the rest of his days.

Vivier returned to Paris after two years to do military service, but crossed the Atlantic again in 1940 as soon as he was demobilized. He sailed from Lisbon on the *Exeter*, one of the last liners to make the crossing for the duration of the war. On the captain's bridge he met Madame Cuttoli, a leading light of the artistic and literary world in pre-war Paris, while on deck he met Suzanne Rémy, who was to become a good friend and colleague. She was a senior designer of millinery at Agnès, one of the great names in Parisian fashion. She, too, was emigrating, accompanied by her mother.

On arrival in New York, Vivier lost no time in making contact with his old customers and setting up shop on 55th Street. Unhappily, when the United States entered the war, restrictions were imposed, and leather was one of the goods in short supply. He found himself without the basic materials he needed to continue making shoes. While working for Delman part-time, he began to experiment with photography, a 'modern form of expression' which had always appealed to him. He became assistant to Hoyningen-Huene, who worked for *Vogue*, and so renewed his links with the world of fashion. He socialized with many of the European artists in exile in the United States, notably Fernand Léger, Max Ernst, Alexander Calder and Marc Chagall. A few months later, short of money but not short of ideas, the handsome young man with the aristocratic profile turned his attention from women's feet to their heads.

With the assistance of Mademoiselle Rémy, who taught him the nuts and bolts of the trade, Roger Vivier transformed himself in next to no time from designer to milliner. Slicing into felt shapes with no more than his intuition to guide him, he sped through his apprenticeship in less than a year and soon began creating hats of an airy delicacy. 'I worked like a sculptor, directly on the clients' heads. A successful hat is a matter of balance and the way it shades the eyes.' Before long, their shop, Suzanne et Roger, was all the rage on 64th Street. Ambition the two proprietors had in plenty, but little in the way of funds. No matter; they lined the walls with chocolate wrappers and relied for the rest on improvisation. Much pummelling and snipping and scrunching ensued, and out of all this activity there emerged intertwined stems of black lilac, bouquets of feathers, straws, turbans and cartwheel hats with clusters of forget-me-nots wreathed around rippling brims.

Their creations appeared on the covers of all the fashion magazines and their quintessentially French boutique was pronounced one of *the* places to see, and to be seen in, in New York. Vivier derived from these years an inimitable style and technique, of which he was fiercely proud. 'Can't you see the milliner in that?' he demanded one day in 1987, indicating a black-satin shoe with heel 'trimmed' in white organdie. He was opening the retrospective of his work, 'Les Souliers de Roger Vivier', held at the Musée des Arts de la Mode in Paris.

retrospective. The word makes sense in the context of an artist who has now come to the end of a long and productive life, and whose designs are housed in the most famous museums in the world (The Metropolitan Museum of Art in New York, the Victoria and Albert Museum in London), yet it sits ill with the image of a man who never rested on his laurels but always led his life in the present. 'I recently visited the Musée des Arts de la Mode in Paris. They have a display of my designs. They are perfectly fine, but I can't imagine myself now designing such elaborate shoes. When you're young, you just don't realize. I've made some pretty things, but nothing perfect!'

For Roger Vivier, modesty and high standards went hand in hand. And he was always in search of something new and daring – that, indeed, was how he liked to see himself. Take, for example, the sandal called *Vague* (Wave) with the all-in-one plastic sole and heel, which he invented in 1997 in one last dazzling demonstration of his technical virtuosity. 'I have always been passionate about line. I have revised my designs five hundred times to test whether an idea is right and whether it respects the architecture of the foot.' His work is, and will remain, an inexhaustible source of joyous inspiration for the generations to come who want to follow in his footsteps, although one suspects the tousled white-haired genius will always remain one step ahead.

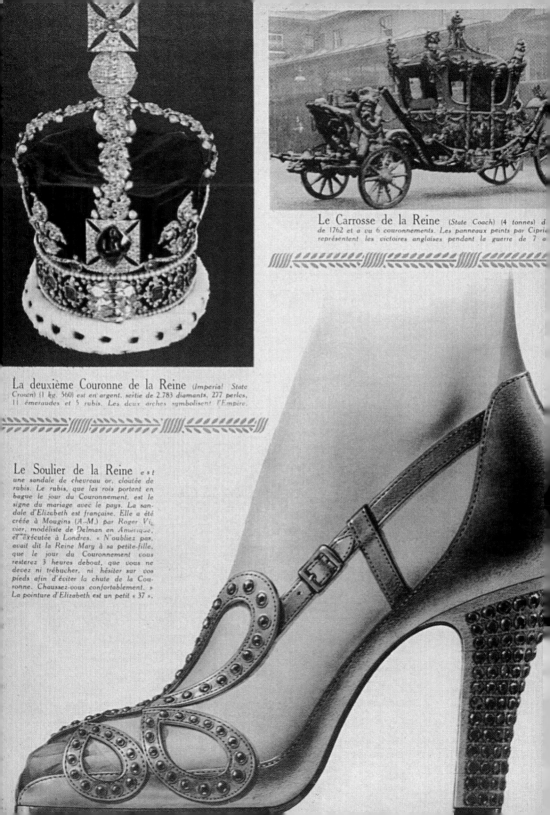

La deuxième Couronne de la Reine (Imperial State Crown) (1 kg. 560) est en argent, sertie de 2.783 diamants, 277 perles, 11 émeraudes et 5 rubis. Les deux arches symbolisent l'Empire.

Le Carrosse de la Reine (State Coach) (4 tonnes) d[...] de 1762 et a vu 6 couronnements. Les panneaux peints par Cipri[...] représentent les victoires anglaises pendant la guerre de 7 a[...]

Le Soulier de la Reine est une sandale de chevreau or, cloutée de rubis. Le rubis, que les rois portent en bague le jour du Couronnement, est le signe du mariage avec le pays. La sandale d'Elizabeth est française. Elle a été créée à Mougins (A.-M.) par Roger Vivier, modéliste de Delman en Amérique, et éxécutée à Londres. « N'oubliez pas, avait dit la Reine Mary à sa petite-fille, que le jour du Couronnement vous resterez 3 heures debout, que vous ne devez ni trébucher, ni hésiter sur vos pieds afin d'éviter la chute de la Couronne. Chaussez-vous confortablement. » La pointure d'Elizabeth est un petit « 37 ».

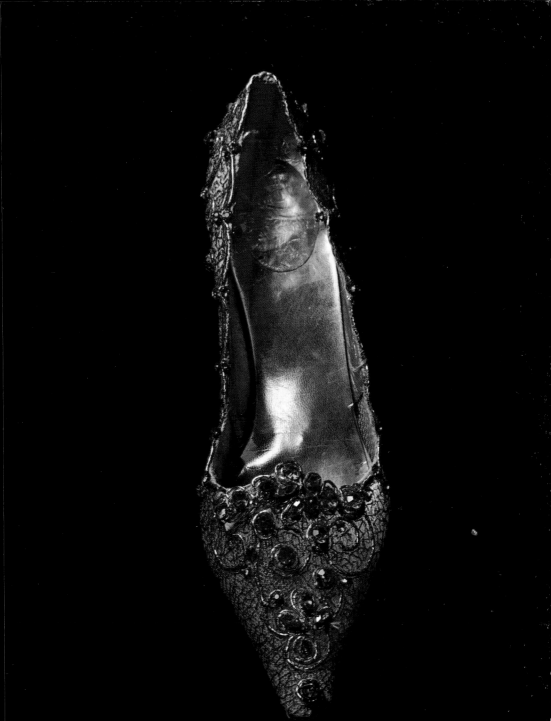

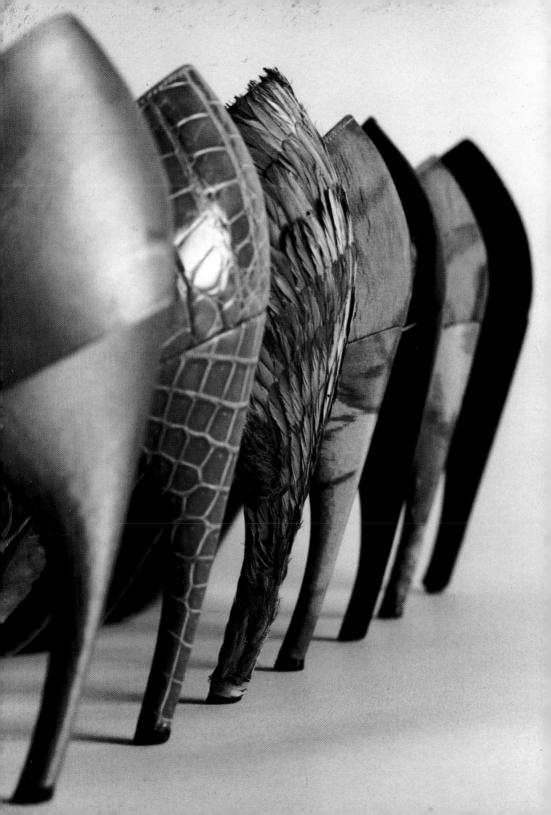

Roger Vivier 1937

DESIGNED BY
Roger Vivier

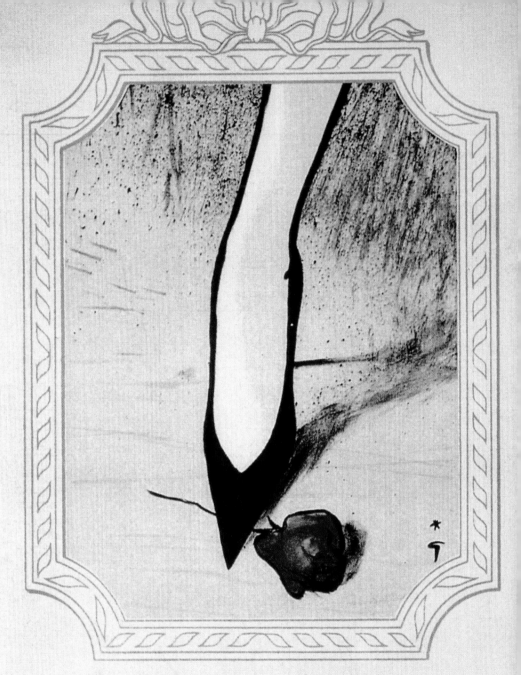

Christian Dior

Souliers créés par

Roger Vivier

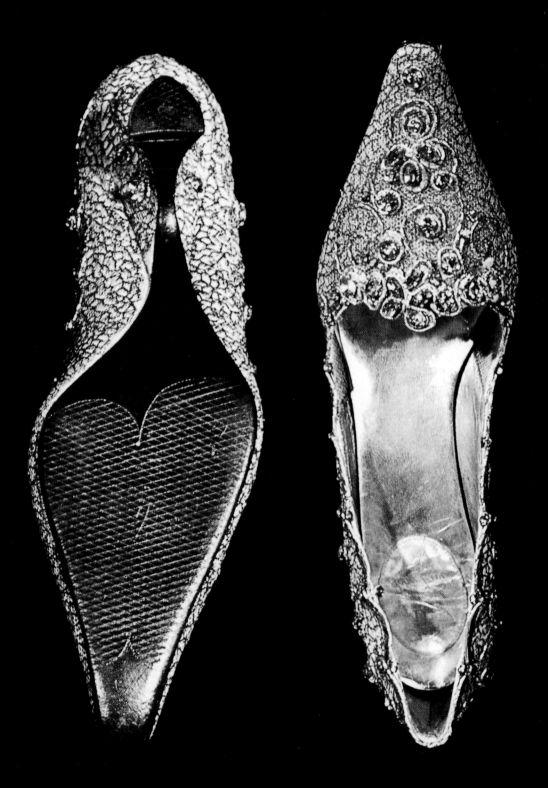

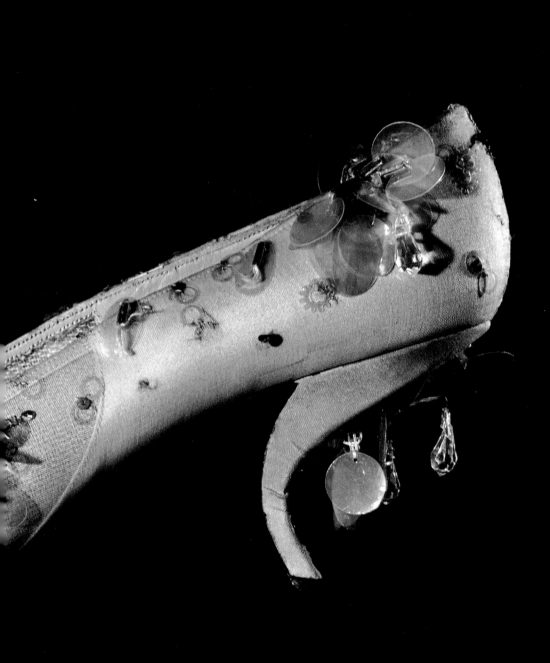

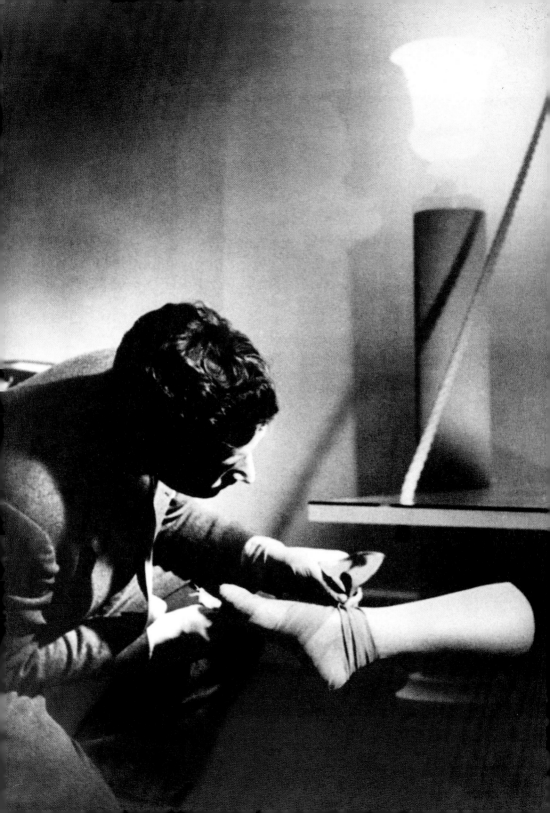

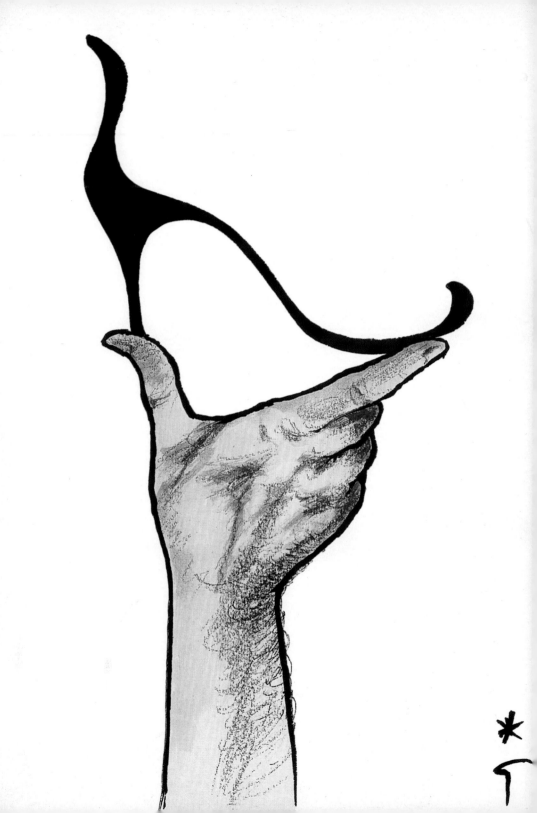

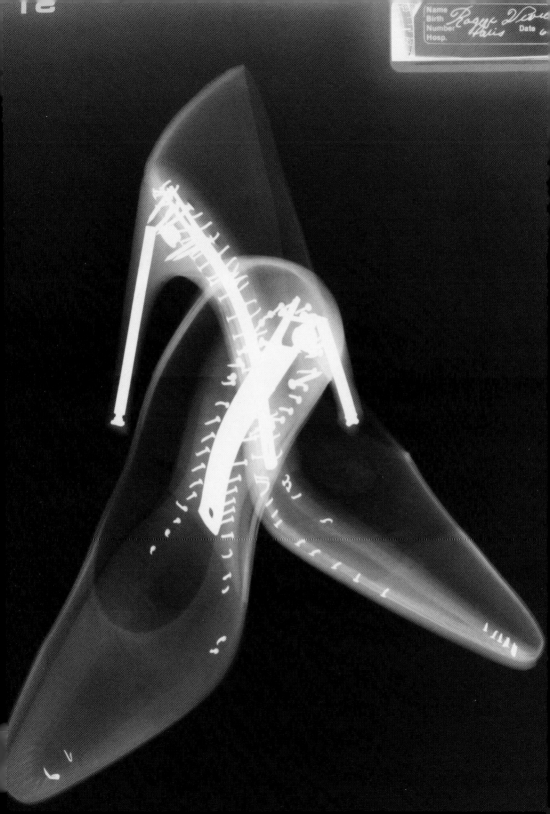

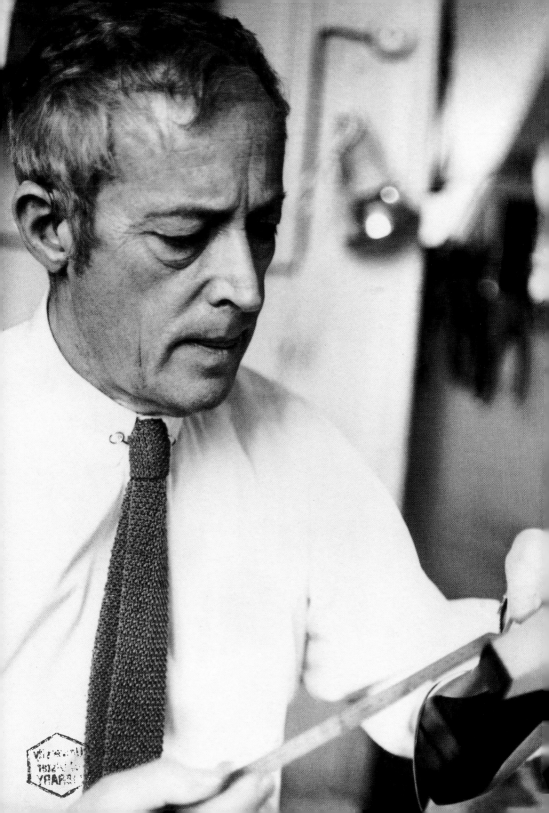

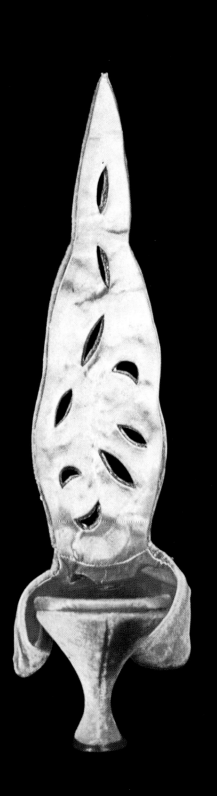

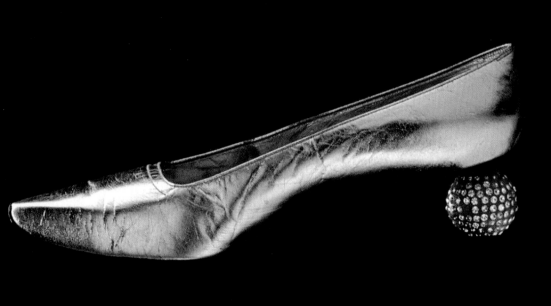

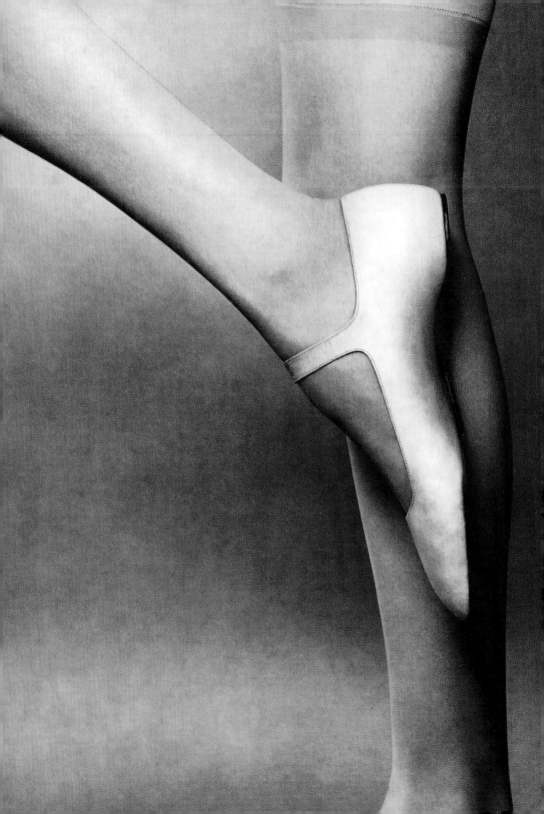

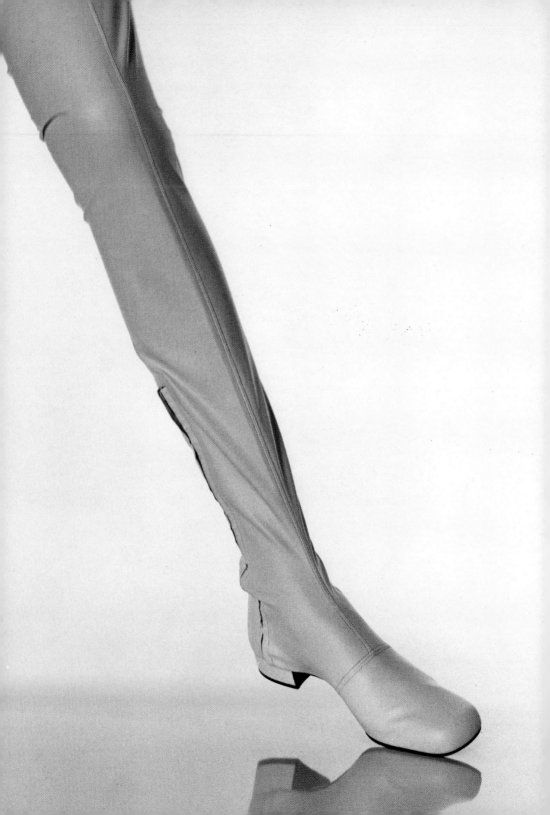

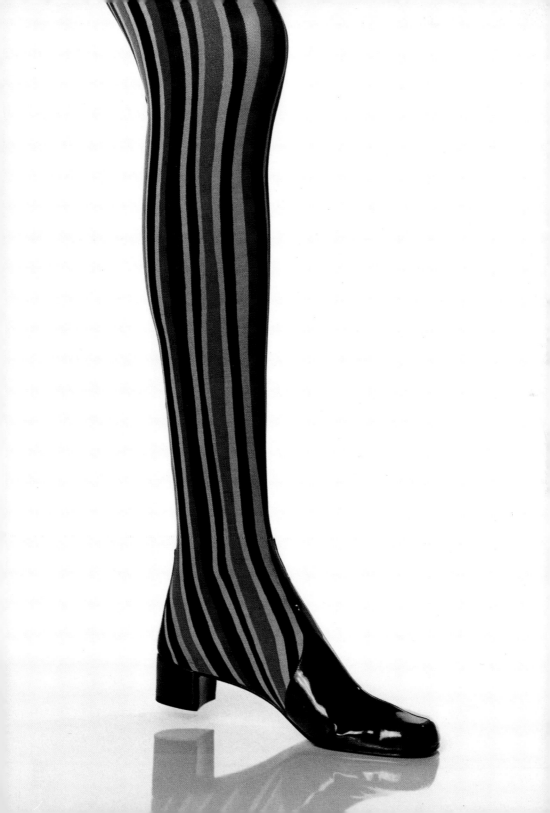

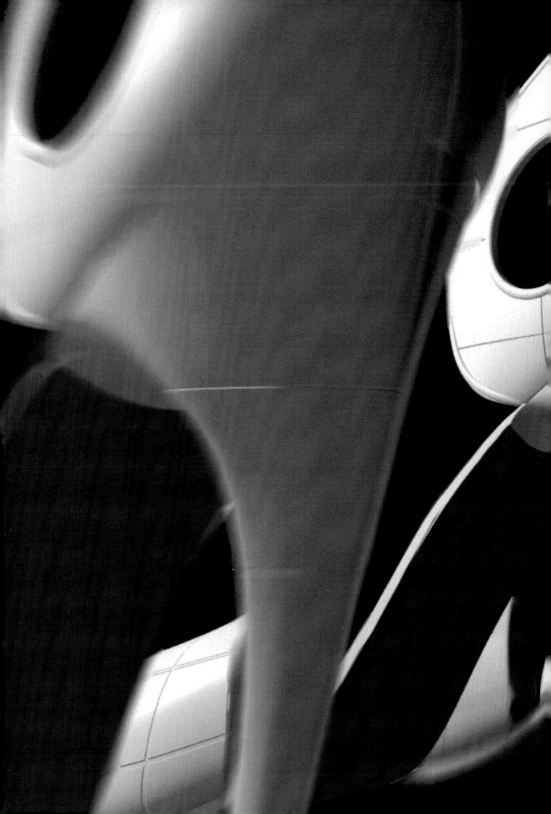

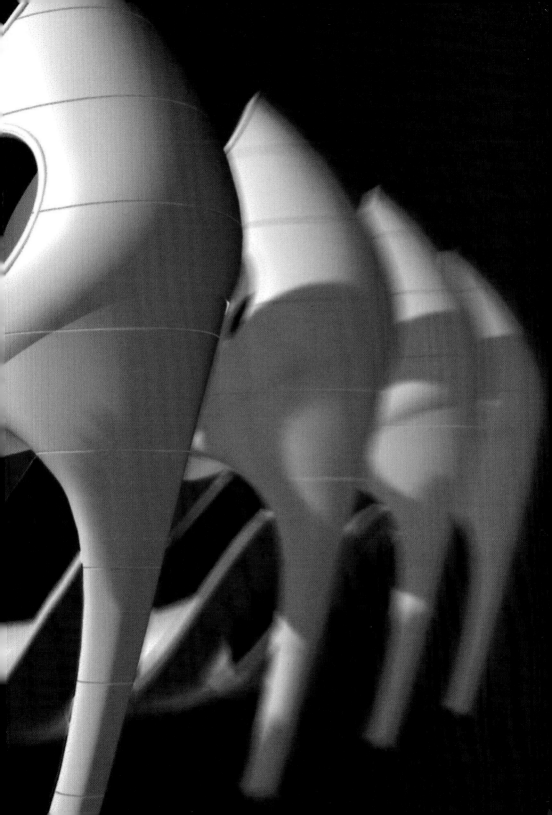

Chronology

1907   13 November, birth of Roger Vivier in Paris.

1916   Aged nine, suffers the loss of both parents.

1925   Enrols at the Ecole des Beaux-Arts, Paris, intending to become a sculptor. Out of the blue, family friends who own a shoe factory suggest he submit designs. These prove so successful that he decides to leave art school and abandon sculpture, and instead learn the craft of shoemaking.

1927   Rather than enrolling at a technical college, Roger Vivier chooses to work in factories and learn the trade from the bottom up. 'The advantage was undoubtedly being able to discover the basics empirically, forms that are as old as the world itself, which I subsequently combined and presented in my own way.'

1936   He is hired by Laboremus, a French sales subsidiary of a big German leather manufacturer, with the brief of forecasting future trends, and so finds himself dictating to powerful industrialists the colours that will be in vogue in coming seasons.

1937   Vivier opens his own workshops at 22, Rue Royale in Paris, and designs for some of the most famous shoe manufacturers in the world: Pinet and Bally in France, Salamander and Mercedes in Germany, Rayne and Turner in England, Miller and Delman in the US.

1939   Called up for military service.

1940   After demobilization, Vivier accepts an offer of employment in America. Catches the last train through Spain to Lisbon, where he embarks on the *Exeter*, one of the last liners to be able to make the transatlantic crossing.

1941   Following the Japanese attack on the American base at Pearl Harbor, the United States enters the war. Economic recession begins to bite, and a law is passed forbidding the manufacture of all new models of shoes. Roger Vivier is obliged to reinvent himself. With the assistance of Suzanne Rémy, former chief milliner at the famous Parisian establishment Agnès, he sets himself to master the art of making hats.

1942   With Mademoiselle Rémy, he opens the hat shop Suzanne et Roger on 64th Street, near the corner with Madison Avenue, New York. For fashionable New Yorkers, it offers the authentic flavour of Paris.

1945   The war over, Vivier returns to shoe design. He is the first to use clear plastic as a material for footwear.

1947   Back in Paris, he is introduced by draughtsman Maurice Van Moppès to Christian Dior.

Roger Vivier, photographed at the Château d'Aubeterre, as he puts the finishing touches to the models intended for the retrospective of his work, 'Les Souliers de Roger Vivier', staged in 1987 at the Musée des Arts de la Mode, Paris. Thigh boot in yellow satin with 'Mimosa' embroidery, made by Lesage. © Photo: François Halard.

1953	Dior expands his empire to include a shoe department and takes on Roger Vivier as designer. Their made-to-measure shoes are so successful that, after two years, they have the idea of moving into ready-to-wear. It is the first time a Paris couturier has joined forces with a shoemaker in a venture aimed at the mass market.
1953–1963	Roger Vivier designs all of Christian Dior's shoes. These ten years represent a golden age of shoe design, with Paris its unrivalled capital.
1963	Sets up his own business in the Rue François Ier, Paris. Launches a new and influential line of shoes with metal buckles mounted, not high on the foot as in the seventeenth century, but low over the toes. Other innovations include the comfortable, square-toed shoe with the lower boot-style heel, plus a thousand and one other models sold all over the world.
1987	In Paris, the Musée des Arts de la Mode stages a retrospective of Roger Vivier's work.
1993	Retrospectives at the Musée Internationale de la Chaussure in Romans-sur-Isère (Drôme) and at the Museum of Decorative Arts, Helsinki (Finland).
1995	Retrospective in Taipei (Taiwan), arranged by the *Ming Sheng Daily*. Exhibition 'Autour de Roger Vivier' at the Galerie Enrico-Navarra, Paris.
1996	Designs for Agnès B.
1997	His paper cutouts are the subject of an exhibition staged by Les Editions Serge Aboukrat, Paris. Retrospective in Tokyo at Art Gunza Space, arranged by Shiseido.
1998	2 October, Roger Vivier dies in Toulouse at the age of ninety.

Roger Vivier has been the recipient of the Neiman Marcus 'Oscar', the Daniel Fisher Award and the Prix Tibère. His shoes are in the collections of The Metropolitan Museum of Art, New York; the Victoria and Albert Museum, London; the Musée de la Mode et du Costume de la Ville de Paris, the Palais Galliera, and the Musée des Arts de la Mode in the Palais du Louvre, Paris.

Sandal, 1996. The heel and sole of clear plastic, moulded in one piece, form a single entity. This model is evidence both of Roger Vivier's stylistic consistency and of his ability to adapt to the mood of the times. © Archives Roger Vivier.

Roger Vivier

Gold kid-skin sandal studded with garnets (resembling rubies), 1953. 'Liturgical' shoe for the coronation of Queen Elizabeth II of England. Drawing: Roger Vivier. Archives Roger Vivier. © All rights reserved. **High-heeled evening shoe** mounted on nylon mesh with 'goat's foot' heel, 1962. Silver-thread embroidery on tulle, artificial topazes. Photo: Jean-Louis Benoit. © Archives Roger Vivier.

Satin, crocodile, even kingfisher feathers (this fabulous shoe is in The Metropolitan Museum of Art, New York), the immaculate arch of the '*choc*' heel lends itself to every conceivable variation. © Photo: Cynthia Hampton, 1988. **Roger Vivier in 1933**, Place Vendôme, Paris. At the time, he was working at the nearby offices of Laboremus, the Paris subsidiary of a German leather manufacturer, which had hired him to modernize its range. © Archives Roger Vivier.

The window of Bergdorf Goodman, New York, 1955. The display at the luxury Fifth Avenue store features a formal evening dress by Christian Dior and a range of shoes designed by Roger Vivier under the brand name Delman-Christian Dior, in use from 1953 to 1955. Photo: Archives Roger Vivier. © All rights reserved.

Drawing by René Gruau, 1960. Advertisement for shoes created by Roger Vivier for Christian Dior. Gruau's elegant draughtsmanship perfectly conveys the shoe's purity of line as well as the sophistication of the age. © René Gruau/Archives Sylvie Nissen. **Roger Vivier in conversation with Suzanne Luling**, in charge of public relations for Christian Dior, in the salon of the fashion house in the Avenue Montaigne, Paris, in 1955. Photo: Archives Roger Vivier. © All rights reserved.

Under construction. The upper of this made-to-measure shoe is photographed here together with the wooden last on which it is built, 1956. Archives Roger Vivier. © Photo: André Ostier.

'**Cobblers make shoes** so you don't have to go about barefoot. But Roger Vivier is the couturier of the woman's foot; he is its milliner, its furrier and its jeweller. On the heel, ankle, scaphoid and metatarsals of that foot, he puts a shoe that is at once dress and coat, hairstyle and jewelry. To the point that a woman shod by Roger Vivier who went out for a walk stark naked would still appear to be very much dressed.' (James de Coquet, 1980.) © Photo: André Ostier.

High-heeled evening shoe, 1962. Silver-thread embroidery on tulle with artificial topazes, mounted on nylon mesh. The sole is as significant here as the embroidery on the upper, its complex shape demonstrating the skill involved in the design and its execution. Photo: Jean-Louis Benoit. © Archives Roger Vivier. **High-heeled shoe**, 1963. Satin and tulle, with embroideries of mother-of-pearl spangles and 'comma' heel. Photo: Jean-Louis Benoit. © Archives Roger Vivier.

High-heeled shoe, 1963. Satin and tulle, with embroideries of mother-of-pearl spangles and 'comma' heel. 'That bouquet of teardrops made of shards of mica, more muted than crystal … what is that? From Roger Vivier, so reserved and self-effacing, comes only the muttered response: "It's Cinderella's chandelier, the evening before the ball, before it lights up in her honour…".' (Violette Leduc, *Vogue*, March 1965.) Photo: Jean-Louis Benoit. © Archives Roger Vivier.

High-heeled fabric shoe with square toe, with draped satin rose on the upper, 1965. Photo: Jean-Louis Benoit. © Archives Roger Vivier. **Roger Vivier fastening a strap around a client's ankle**, at his made-to-measure workshop on the Rue Royale, Paris, 1937. Photo: Brassaï. © Gilberte Brassaï.

Cutaway embroidered evening shoe with ankle fastenings and stiletto heel with rectangular base, marked '*Christian Dior et Roger Vivier*', 1956. This model is very much of its times, the counterpart of the famous furniture that Ero Saarinen designed for Knoll, or of Le Corbusier's concrete chapel at Ronchamp. Archives Roger Vivier. © Photo: André Ostier.

Much in vogue between 1956 and 1959 was this narrow elongated toe, either square or concave at the tip. It is utterly characteristic in style of the period that Edmonde Charles-Roux has called the golden age of *haute couture*. Photo: William Klein, 1956. © Courtesy *Vogue* US, The Condé Nast Publications, Inc., 1958, renewed in 1986.

High-heeled shoe with crossover straps in green chiné taffeta, with '*choc*' heel, 1959. The sole item of decoration is the rhinestone ball that serves as a button. Photo: Jean-Louis Benoit. © Archives Roger Vivier.

In this 1956 model, the heel is positioned underneath the ball of the foot. The back of the heel is spatula-shaped and decorated with rhinestones, while the upper is left plain. © Photo: André Ostier. **High-heeled day shoe in crocodile with 'prow' heel**, 1957. A small miracle of equilibrium, this model was designed for ease of walking. Made in crocodile and in calfskin, it represented the peak of Parisian elegance during the fifties. © Photo: André Ostier.

Infinite variations by Roger Vivier on the silhouette of the court shoe. Archives Roger Vivier. © Photo: André Ostier. **Satin high-heeled shoe** with silver silk thread and rhinestone embroideries, with four embroidered flowers on the cutaway front and sides, and straight-cut stiletto heel, 1956. © Photo: Cynthia Hampton.

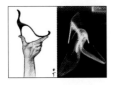

Drawing by René Gruau, 1995. A man's hand supports the 'idealized' silhouette of a Roger Vivier creation. Archives Roger Vivier. © René Gruau. *The Bride Stripped Bare*, Steve Miller, 1995. Screen print and acrylic on canvas (101 x 76 cm). Shown as part of the exhibition 'Autour de Roger Vivier' staged by Serge Aboukrat in 1995 at the Galerie Enrico-Navarra, Paris. © Steve Miller.

Harper's Bazaar was the first of the fashion magazines to pick up on the '*choc*' heel, with a description in March 1959 of Roger Vivier's latest invention. Archives Roger Vivier. © Photo: André Ostier. **Satin high-heeled shoe with pointed toe**, 1956. The stiletto heel is a perfect vertical with an imperious profile. © Photo: André Ostier.

Lamé evening shoe with stiletto heel and tapered toe, upturned at the tip, 1962. © Photo: André Ostier.

Two paper cutouts by Roger Vivier, 1992 (64 x 50 cm). During the nineties, Roger Vivier produced several series of coloured paper cutouts featuring the archetypal silhouettes of his designs. These two works were shown in the exhibition staged by Les Editions Serge Aboukrat in Paris in 1997. © Archives Roger Vivier.

Roger Vivier in his workshop in the Rue François Ier, Paris, c. 1960. © Archives Roger Vivier. **Evening mule**, 1962. Velvet studded with jewels. 'Roger Vivier's evening shoes are the works of a jeweller rather than a shoemaker. Only empresses and queens of the screen can indulge in them.' (*L'Aurore*, February 1962.) Photo: Jean-Louis Benoit. © Archives Roger Vivier.

Models embroidered by Lesage, created for the exhibition 'Les Souliers de Roger Vivier' at the Musée des Arts de la Mode, Paris, in 1987. The keynote is transparency, in both construction and decoration, with lace cleverly combined with crystal embroideries. © Photo: Roland Beaufre, 1987. **Black-suede high-heeled shoe**, 1988. The ornamental scroll mounted on the upper mirrors the shape of the arch as it extends through into the '*choc*' heel. © Photo: Cynthia Hampton.

The Ghost Shoe (*L'escarpin fantôme*), X-ray by Henri Terres (detail), 1995. Gelatin on polyester (23.7 x 27.7 cm). This work was displayed at the Galerie Enrico-Navarra, Paris, as part of the exhibition 'Autour de Roger Vivier' staged by Serge Aboukrat in 1995. © Archives Roger Vivier. **Paper cutout** by Roger Vivier, shown at the exhibition staged by Les Editions Serge Aboukrat in Paris in 1997. © Archives Roger Vivier.

Strappy sandal in watered silk, with stiletto heel and sharply pointed toe, 1967. Archives Roger Vivier. © Photo: André Ostier.

Satin high-heeled shoe, with 'prow' heel, 1958. This heel made its first appearance in late 1957: slightly broader where it meets the ground, it then narrows in mid-shaft. The back of the heel forms a sharp vertical angle. Archives Roger Vivier. © Photo: André Ostier.

Gold kid-skin shoe with pointed, upturned toe and plastic heel in the form of a ball encrusted with rhinestones, 1966 (above). **Pink-satin mule** embroidered with rhinestones, with Louis XV 'patten' and 6 cm hollow heel; bevelled toe in black leather (below). Musée de la Mode et du Costume de la Ville de Paris. © Photo: Jacques Boulay. **An Oriental fantasy of the love generation**, in which Cinderella wears transparent vinyl. Photo: Norman Parkinson, 1966. © Elle/Scoop.

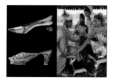

'Baby shoe', from the range called 'In Movement', 1965. The heel is concealed within the shoe, and the sole alone appears to echo the arch of the foot. Photo: Guy Bourdin. © Samuel Bourdin. **Pop Art shoe**, 1967. Patent sandal with platform sole and 'tube' heel. A modern version of the built-up shoes of the forties. In his collection of that year, Yves Saint Laurent teamed his day and evening suits with platform-soled sandals of this type. Photo: Guy Bourdin. © Samuel Bourdin.

Thigh boot in ginza, 1967. Short zip on the inside leg. The press were enthusiastic about ginza: 'It's a material that comes from Japan, as supple as silk and as alive as leather, which climbs right up the leg...'. (*Le Nouvel Observateur*, 27 October 1967.) Archives Roger Vivier. © All rights reserved. **Stocking-shoe in chestnut-brown patent leather** and elasticated fabric, with tapering upper and hollow 'stumpy' heel, 1968. Archives Roger Vivier. © All rights reserved.

Black patent shoe with square boot-style heel, low-cut upper and broad metal buckle, designed to accompany Yves Saint Laurent's collection of July 1965. Photo: Jean-Louis Benoit. © Archives Roger Vivier. **An Yves Saint Laurent outfit** teamed with Roger Vivier's famous 'Pilgrim pumps'. 'The extreme elegance of his shoes added the defining touch to the line of my dresses.' (Yves Saint Laurent.) Photo: Guy Bourdin; from *Vogue* France, March 1966. © Samuel Bourdin.

High-heeled shoe in lilac-coloured velvet decorated with a bunch of violets, with square toe and straight heel, 1966. Photo: Jean-Louis Benoit. © Archives Roger Vivier. White-satin sandal with strap decorated with a pink-satin rose and pyramid heel, 1969. This new heel is triangular in section at the base and narrower at the top, where it joins the simple support on which the foot rests. Photo: Jean-Louis Benoit. © Archives Roger Vivier.

Shoe cupboard (detail) belonging to the Duchess of Windsor, one of Roger Vivier's most loyal customers. © Mohammed Al Fayed. Openwork shoe in fuchsia-pink crêpe de Chine, with square toe and 'goat's foot' heel. Musée Yves Saint Laurent, Paris. © Photo: Cynthia Hampton.

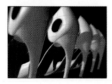

The 'choc' heel, invented by Roger Vivier in 1959, was Ito Morabito's inspiration for this Futuristic array of synthesized images, 1998. © Ora-Ito.

The publishers are greatly indebted to the late Roger Vivier, Gérard Benoit-Vivier and Henri Terres for their assistance in producing this book.

We also wish to thank Roland Beaufre, Jacques Boulay, René Gruau, François Halard, Cynthia Hampton, William Klein, Ito Morabito and Norman Parkinson.

Finally, our thanks are due also to Samuel Bourdin, Gilberte Brassaï, Lisa Diaz (*Vogue* US), Mohammed Al Fayed, Catherine Fonquerne (Elle/Scoop), Thomas Gunther, Madame Kolesnikoff, Sylvie Nissen, Adrien Ostier, Yvonamor Palix (Espace d'Art Yvonamor Palix, Paris, Mexico), Nathalie Prat (Galerie Enrico-Navarra, Paris) and Amanda Stücklin (Sotheby's, London).